JAK

CARTOONS No. 24

from

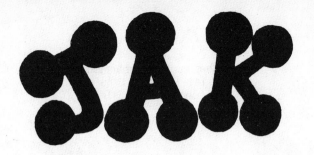 Evening Standard

and

The Mail ON SUNDAY

CHAPMANS

Chapmans Publishers Ltd
141–143 Drury Lane
London WC2B 5TB

First published by Chapmans 1992

ISBN 1 85592 731 4

Printed and bound in Great Britain by
Clays Ltd, St Ives plc.

October 7, 1991

The Rugby World Cup was being held in London.

"Pull your stomach in, Sidney, or people will think your're one of those awful prop forwards!"

October 9, 1991

As part of the Great Japan Exhibition in London, a team of giant sumo wrestlers, here to perform at the Royal Albert Hall, captured the public's imagination.

"It's not a love note, Glenda, they just want to sign you up for a six-month tour of Japan!"

October 10, 1991

A plan was suggested to administer on-the-spot fines for school children's misdemeanours.

"That'll be £1 for chewing, £2 for smoking, and I'll have to ask the Head how much for the other!"

The Milan fashion collections were particularly *risqué* this year.

"Is that something from the Milan collection, Cynthia, or have you forgotten to put a frock on?"

October 15, 1991

Just how far would the
proposed cuts in military
spending go?

"I really think you're worrying too much about these army cuts, Charles!"

October 16, 1991

The winners of the TV franchise battle were announced, and there were notable losers, including TV-am and Thames.

"... And now we interrupt this programme with a terribly important announcement!"

October 18, 1991

Richard Branson was pictured upending Ivana Trump in a publicity stunt at a party in London.

"I was going to fly Virgin until I saw the way they treated the First Class passengers!"

Prince Charles's plan to build the "model village" of Poundbury as an extension of the town of Dorchester was strongly criticized by local and professional opposition. Poundbury was meant to exemplify the Prince's notion of good architecture, to roll back 50 years of disastrous planning and put heart back into English towns and cities.

"... And the pub dates all the way back to last Monday!"

October 23, 1991

The Royal Opera House put up "closed" signs as a bitter row with its orchestra escalated. Musicians were told to go home after they banned overtime and appeared for one performance in jeans and T-shirts instead of evening dress.

"Hold it ladies! I think we'll leave the spoons out for the first act of La Traviata!"

The House of Lords decreed that a woman has the right to refuse her husband inside marriage. The landmark judgment threw out a 250-year-old legal principle that there is no such thing as rape within marriage.

"Hang on Jimmy, I think I've changed my mind!"

High street banks came in for more criticism, this time for their treatment of small businesses.

"That scarecrow looks uncannily like the local bank manager"

October 29, 1991

Prime Minister John Major launched a campaign called Opportunity 2000 aimed at clearing a path through the obstacles that stop women breaking into top jobs through the so-called "glass ceiling".

"I have decided to break the 'glass ceiling' and appoint a woman to the Board . . . I believe most of you know my wife!"

October 31, 1991

Prime Minister John Major introduced a Patient's Charter to limit the waiting time for operations.

"He's been waiting nearly half an hour!"

Tickets for the World Rugby Cup Final between England and Australia were changing hands for a fortune.

"William's working himself into a frenzy for the World Rugby Cup!"

November 4, 1991

It was revealed that England's fearsome rugby hooker Brian Moore had switched career from a solicitor to a financial consultant.

"Perhaps you'd prefer a financial adviser who doesn't play for England?"

November 5, 1991

Prince Charles's favourite hunt – the Leicestershire Quorn – was caught on video by the League Against Cruel Sports when they dug a fox cub from its earth and released it to the hounds which ripped it to pieces. The hunt's chairman and four joint masters resigned.

"They 'ad to give up foxhunting because of the bad publicity"

Coronation Street star Bill Roach won £50,000 in a libel case against the Sun newspaper which had wrongly accused him of being smug, boring and dull.

"Has the Coronation Street case ended yet?"

November 8, 1991

Chancellor Norman
Lamont announced an
extra £11 billion for public
services.

"Hang on everybody, I've got some good news about the bedpans!"

November 10, 1991

The level of British Rail delays, cancellations, technical failures and feeble excuses reached a new high.

"You never hear of leaves on the line stopping trains on the Continent"

November 11, 1991

Director of Public Prosecutions, Sir Allan Green, resigned after being arrested for kerb crawling.

"I think they're in training for the DPP's job!"

Madonna lived up to her reputation as pop's material girl when she clinched an estimated billion-dollar deal with entertainment and publishing giant Time-Warner.

"If you only could sing, Vera!"

November 14, 1991

British Rail boss Bob Reid
appeared in public with a
burly minder, nicknamed
Mr T.

"I see Bob Reid's making a second visit to Basildon!"

November 15, 1991

Millions of bottles of Lucozade were withdrawn from the shelves after animal rights campaigners claimed to have contaminated supplies.

"By Jove, that Lucozade's got a bit of a kick in it!"

November 18, 1991

The issue of Scottish devolution made the news again. This cartoon upset 16 Labour MPs who spoke out against it, describing it as "an insult to Scots".

"Do I put Norman Lamont's name on the deportation list if Scotland gets devolution?"

November 19, 1991

Share prices on the Stock Market fell sharply.

"Could your investment broker ring you back madam, he's having confidence rebuilding therapy?"

After Terry Waite was released by his Lebanese captors he talked of receiving a postcard from someone he did not know, depicting John Bunyon in Bedford Jail. This, he said, helped give him strength to endure his capture.

"I 'ad a postcard once, one of those dirty ones from Brighton!"

November 25, 1991

Former premier Margaret Thatcher had infuriated Prime Minister John Major by making an anti-Europe speech in the Commons.

CONSERVATIVE PRIVATE MEETING

"... Then Algy told her, in the interests of the party, and the country, she should lie back and think of England!"

JAK

November 26, 1991

The great Europe debate was getting a little out of hand. But, to some, it didn't matter that much.

"Harry's worried sick about going into Europe!"

A group of supermarket chains announced they were going to flout Sunday trading laws by opening seven days a week during the run-up to Christmas.

"I don't think it's another Harvest Festival, Doris. It's the vicar competing with Tesco's!"

December 2, 1991

Several supermarket chains defied Sunday trading laws and stayed open seven days a week.

"Looks like he tried to stop the rush to the supermarkets!"

December 3, 1991

Richard Branson
announced he wanted to
start his own railway.

"British Rail announce the arrival of the 8.15 Virgin Express now landing on platform two!"

December 4, 1991

Members of the world's athletics fraternity expressed disquiet about sex tests involving "visual inspection of genitalia". The controversy arose in Australia, where it was said the new tests would not solve the problem of a man who had had a sex change and was running as a woman.

"As a compromise Kylie, we'll allow you to run in the men's hundred yards, if you'll give them a ten-yard start!"

December 6, 1991

The scale of Robert
Maxwell's financial
deception was revealed.
Some £500 million was
missing from the dead
tycoon's business empire.

"It's nice to know you can take it with you!"

December 8, 1991

Sunday trading became reality for supermarkets – and a nightmare for the church.

December 9, 1991

Speculation was rife about the imminent sale of Robert Maxwell's Mirror newspapers after the collapse of many of his debt-ridden companies.

"Of course, you'd have to maintain its traditional image!"

December 10, 1991

At the Maastricht Summit, John Major clashed with other European leaders over everything from the single Euro currency to plans to hand back power to the unions.

"It's just like Arnhem, except we're more outnumbered this time!"

December 11, 1991

Royal catering firm Town and Country crashed with debts of £10 million. The company was the chosen supplier for the Queen's three summer garden parties.

"Could you do a few more sandwiches for the garden party, the caterers have gone bust!"

December 12, 1991

Besieged by newspapermen at his home after hearing an appeal against the seizure of Kevin Maxwell's passport, the presiding judge shielded his face with a briefcase and was alleged to have kicked a taxi driver and a photographer. He later said he regretted the incident.

"May I say what a brilliantly well-judged place kick, your honour!"

December 18, 1991

In a break with protocol, the Government announced the name of the new boss of MI5. What was more, it was a woman, Stella Rimington.

"All right this time, Bond, but in future I give the orders!"

December 19, 1991

The chill wind of recession was blowing through Britain's Christmas celebrations.

"What an office party! One bottle of wine and a bag of crisps – I suppose sex is out of the question?"

December 20, 1991

A City broker won her case for constructive dismissal from her £150,000 a year job. She accused her boss of not awarding her agreed bonuses after returning from maternity leave.

"You may be a lousy money broker, Jones, but at least you don't get pregnant!"

December 27, 1991

The post-Christmas sales got off to a less-than-brisk start.

"One really has to pamper the queues these days!"

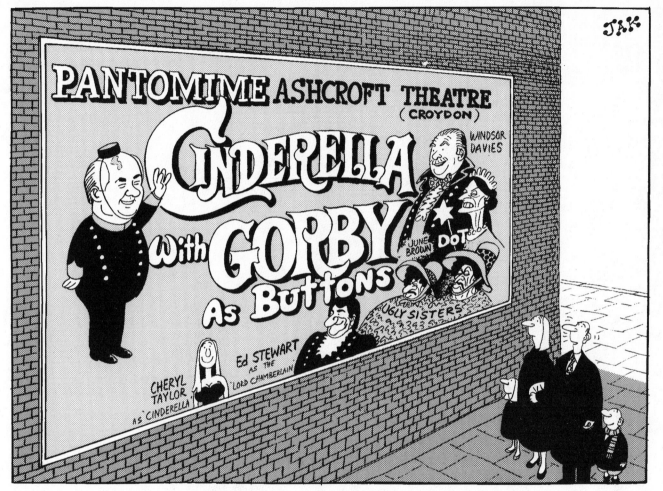

December 29, 1991

Soviet Premier Mikhail Gorbachev was out of a job when the USSR split to become the Commonwealth of Independent States.

"It's only until he gets a proper job!"

December 30, 1991

Rumours about exactly how British Rail would be privatised continued.

"... At Liverpool you change to Virgin Rail till you get to Crewe, take the M&S down to Watford, and finish up in Euston on the Orient Express!"

Building-site workers were threatened with the sack if they indulged in sexist pastimes, like wolf-whistling at passing women and sticking up posters of nude women.

"It's about your sexist attitude, Valerie, now you've upset the scaffolders!"

In the New Year's Honours, the Queen awarded the Royal Victorian Order to a gardener, a luggage porter and a coachman.

"Not in the Honours List again I see, Charlie. I'm sure it must be an oversight on the Queen's part!"

January 3, 1992

A report revealed that some high-street exhaust repair shops had sold new exhaust systems which were not needed.

"Kwik-Fit told me the old exhaust system needed changing!"

January 6, 1992

A consignment of British beef aid was refused by the Russians because, they claimed, it was contaminated with "Mad Cow" disease.

"It was only a couple of roubles, but we've got to tell the doctor if we start growing another ear, or losing our tempers!"

January 8, 1992

Figures released showed that tapes and CDs now dominate the UK music market.

"... So he said to me, come up to my place and listen to my LPs. What's an LP I said ...?"

Silicone breast implants were halted following a health scare from America which suggested there were long-term risks from the operation.

"But Fiona's only had half the treatment!"

January 10, 1992

It was announced that Lady Helen Windsor was to marry art dealer Tim Taylor.

"I know how much in love you are Timothy, but would you mind putting Whistler's Mother back in the window!"

January 12, 1992

The annual Crufts dog show began.

"We were told he was a Jack Russell when we bought him as a pup"

January 14, 1992

International publishers scrambled to buy an unfinished book said to reveal the startling sex life of Marlene Dietrich. Little is known of her early life.

"Up till now I'd always thought Fritz had got his scars in the Franco-Prussian War of 1870!"

January 15, 1992

The Maxwell brothers refused to answer questions put to them by a House of Commons committee.

"We almost got a groan out of Kevin!"

Some were dismayed at paintings of the Gulf War by Britain's official war artist. Two works showed Mickey Mouse sitting on a lavatory amid the horrors of war in Kuwait.

"That's one of the colonel in the '91 Gulf War!"

January 17, 1992

A cleaning woman handed over to police 120 holiday photographs of the Duchess of York with American millionaire Steve Wyatt. She found the pictures at the top of a wardrobe in a flat once rented by Wyatt.

"Brilliant work getting the Fergie photos, Carruthers. Now could you do the office before your next assignment!"

January 20, 1992

Northern Ireland Secretary Peter Brooke was accused of being insensitive when he appeared on Irish television and sang "Oh My Darling Clementine" on the same evening as a workers' minibus was blown up by the IRA in Tyrone in Northern Ireland.

"Do I know I'm a bloody fool? No! But if you hum it I'll sing it!"

Police chiefs came under fire from front-line officers who were demanding US-style batons to replace the traditional truncheon.

"Why sergeant, is that a long side-handled baton in your pocket or are you just pleased to see me?"

The Labour Party was forced into an embarrassing retreat when they backed down over a key election pledge that no one earning less than £21,000 would pay more under Labour.

"Strange as it may seem, Sid, I think we could be worse off under Labour!"

January 26, 1992

A Benetton advertisement showing a newly born baby was criticised and some versions were withdrawn.

"I suppose it's a Benetton advert"

January 28, 1992

Elton John finally took off his hat to display a magnificent head of hair. Superstar watchers were asking the question: "Toupee or not toupee?"

"Until it moved I thought it was Elton John's wig!"

January 29, 1992

Prime Minister John Major launched his Citizen's Charter aimed at giving the individual the right to an answer when confronted with inefficiency and unnecessary bureaucracy.

"Let me through, I'm a Citizen's Charter inspector!"

A 17-year-old actress from Pinner, who starred in the film *The Lover*, found herself at the centre of a did-she-didn't-she guessing game when the film's producer claimed she had had intercourse during the "simulated" sex scenes.

"She's from Pinner"

January 31, 1992

Yet again the issue of Scottish independence hit the headlines.

"Ticket! Passport!"

"They came with the car!"

February 11, 1992

A report by Continental Research showed men are aware that having sex with a female boss can increase their promotional prospects and salaries.

"How far do you want to go in the company, Perkins?"

February 12, 1992

World heavyweight boxing champion Mike Tyson was accused of raping a beauty queen in his hotel room at two in the morning. He was later convicted and imprisoned for six years.

"What did you expect when I invited you up to my room at two in the morning? Didn't you know I was a boxer?"

February 14, 1992

Labour MP Kevin McNamara introduced a Bill aimed at protecting mammals. Opponents saw it as an attempt to ban field sports in Britain.

"Bloody Fascist! Leave that maggot alone!"

The Duchess of York was reputedly treated by a clairvoyant who asked her to sit under a glass pyramid designed to relieve stress while treating her for back and neck pain.

"The hunt's ready to move out, m'dear. Do you feel calm enough to face the saboteurs yet?"

Lloyd's insurers predicted massive losses for some of its syndicates.

The man who applied to be a Name at Lloyd's!

February 20, 1992

London crime figures
showed a huge rise,
particularly in car crime.

February 21, 1992

Sara Keays won £105,000 in libel damages from *New Woman* magazine for an article wrongly calling her a "kiss and tell bimbo".

"Goodbye Miss Keays, it's always a pleasure to see you!"

February 23, 1992

Pop superstar Michael Jackson was swamped by fans when he arrived to stay at the Dorchester Hotel in Park Lane.

"They've torn the first decoy to pieces. Now let's try Plan B"

February 26, 1992

Rolls-Royce lost £60 million in 1991 after its toughest trading year.

"But I don't want to buy another Rolls-Royce!"

February 27, 1992

Lord Justice Taylor was named as the new Lord Chief Justice after the early retirement of Lord Lane. "We must make the judiciary seem more user-friendly," he said.

"I'd be careful how you shake up the judiciary, Peter; some of them haven't been stirred for years!"

Losses to banks and
building societies soared
to £150 million.

"In the old days they just sent you a letter if you were overdrawn!"

Australian Prime Minister Paul Keating was accused of insulting the Queen when he put his arm around her during an official royal visit. Keating's wife also did not perform the customary curtsey.

"Must you wear that hat, Matilda? I've told everybody you were an East Ender with a speech defect"

March 3, 1992

The 79-metre Ingst bridge was replaced on the M4 – but it took more than 24 hours longer than expected to remove the 2,000-ton structure.

"Never mind the hand signals, Mrs Wilkins – the brakes! Use the BRAKES!!!"

March 4, 1992

The world of film, TV and theatre was in turmoil after a report showed that, on average, actors were paid 30 per cent more than actresses.

"Of course the dummy gets more than you! He's an actor"

March 5, 1992

The RAF's first female Top Gun was suspended from flight combat training after failing the course at RAF Chivenor in Devon.

ROYAL AIR FORCE CHIVENOR

JAK

"... And another thing, Sally, you lose your temper too easily!"

March 6, 1992

New trust hospitals set out to reduce waiting times for patients by cutting out bureaucratic wrangling and lengthy consultations.

"Care for an operation, sir?"

Sir Clive Sinclair launched his environmentally conscious electric bike – the Zike (short for zero emission bicycle).

"It's his lordship's answer to the Sinclair electric bike, but it's the batteries that are the problem!"

John Major launched his election campaign with what his supporters called a giveaway package in the Budget.

"Any news about the Budget yet?"

"Gentlemen, I think we've finally found someone to blame for the Maxwell disaster!"

March 12, 1992

The Budget cuts in car tax highlighted the need to bolster up flagging car sales.

"Yes, there's a long waiting list for this model, would five minutes be too long?"

April 1, 1992

French farmers reacted violently to a fellow Frenchman working for a British firm that imported cheap Turkish onions. In the so-called Onion War a lorry was hijacked and its £32,000 cargo of onions set on fire. Two days later a lorry driver was shot at by angry farmers but escaped injury.

"You must remember me! You burnt my load of Turkish onions in France last week!"

Liberal Democrats were accused of only fielding Paddy Ashdown as the party spokesman.

MASTERMIND TROPHY

"Name three Liberal Democrats apart from Paddy Ashdown?"

April 3, 1992

Neil Kinnock mounted Labour's final push to the polls with a pop-and-politics rally of 8,000 people in Sheffield worthy of an American election convention. Some pundits believe it cost him the election.

The Sheffield Rally

April 6, 1992

The opinion polls
predicted a close-run
election.

"I'm afraid it's election fever – he could go either way!"

". . . And that brute got within six feet of me, just outside Paris!"

April 19, 1992

The United Nations imposed sanctions on all Libyan flights, which were refused landing rights outside her borders. The move was designed to force Colonel Gaddafi to hand over the alleged Lockerbie bombers.

"On landing at Heathrow, passengers are reminded to keep their knees bent and legs close together. Thank you for flying with Libyan Airlines"

April 23, 1992

For Women, the first pornographic magazine for women, went on sale.

April 24, 1992

The Government planned to switch anti-terrorist work from Special Branch to MI5.

" 'Ello, 'ello, 'ello. I'm from MI5!"

April 30, 1992

Francis Bacon died. His work sells for millions.

"I slung all that rubbish out, and scraped all that paint off the walls!"

May 3, 1992

Chief Eurocrat Jacques Delors backed a move to introduce a maximum 48-hour week as part of the Maastricht Treaty. Britain opposed. The battle continues.

"Do stop snivelling, Nigel – the Europeans aren't going to force you to work a 48-hour week"

May 7, 1992

Former world heavyweight boxing champion Mike Tyson, serving a six-year sentence for rape, was said to have threatened prison wardens, saying he would "whip your asses".

"Tyson in solitary again"

May 8, 1992

In a move towards more open government, Prime Minister John Major named Sir Colin McColl as the chief of MI6.

"How humiliating Colin, for years I've been telling people you were a mini-cab driver!"

May 12, 1992

Princess Diana took a holiday in Egypt while Prince Charles headed for Turkey with friends.

"I see Charles and Di are taking separate holidays again!"

May 13, 1992

The Bishop of Galway's lover Anne Murphy claimed that he had offered her hush money to keep quiet both about their affair and their illegitimate son.

"Can I borrow the car dad!"

May 17, 1992

A strike in Germany which affected car production and transport was the first for many years.

"Oh look, Beryl! A lesser German flying picket – you don't see many of those this far west"

May 20, 1992

Satellite TV station BSkyB and the BBC won a joint £304 million, five-year deal for exclusive coverage of Premier League soccer.

"Do you do a discreet sort of dish suitable for a Grade Two listed Elizabethan manor?"

May 21, 1992

British Airways chairman Lord King announced £285 million profits for the airline and reported a 12 per cent boost in productivity brought about by increased workloads and staff cuts. Meanwhile Britain's European partners pushed ahead with plans for a maximum 48-hour week.

"Just answer the question Lord King! Did you or did you not work more than 48 hours last week?"

May 22, 1992

Thailand's dictatorial General Suchinda Kraprayoon was publicly humiliated on television by the country's revered King Bhumibol. The General bowed to the King after he was ordered to introduce democracy and stop killing the country's citizens.

"I've suddenly got an overwhelming desire to see Mrs Thatcher again!"

May 26, 1992

Drought conditions worsened in southern England, particularly in Kent and Sussex.

"Poor Devil, he nearly made it!"

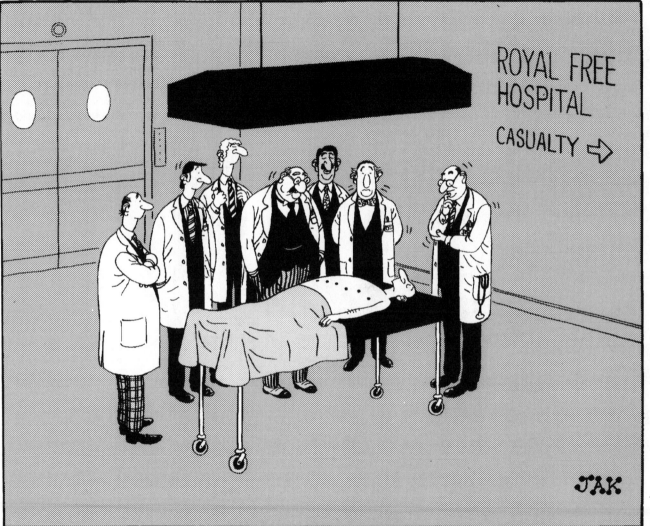

May 28, 1992

A hitman posing as a doctor in a white coat shot and killed patient Graeme Woodhatch at the Royal Free Hospital. Unfortunately doctors did not realise he had been shot four times and the bullet wounds were only noticed when he was in the mortuary five and a half hours after his death.

ROYAL FREE HOSPITAL

CASUALTY ⇨

JAK

"As I suspected, alopecia!"

A 32-year-old Filipino male nurse was claimed to be the world's first man to become pregnant. The man, called Carlo, was born with both male and female sets of reproductive organs. Doctors had surgically removed his male organs before he was said to have become pregnant.

"Let me put it this way, Mr Goldsmith. If it wasn't for a male nurse in the Philippines, you'd have made the Guinness Book of Records!"

June 2, 1992

Prince Charles was accused of "leaning" on supermarket giant Tesco to stop them selling Andrew Morton's controversial book about Princess Diana.

"Of course we dropped it, do you know how much she spends here every day?"

June 4, 1992

Civil servants were told they were being relocated to the ailing Canary Wharf project in Docklands – but the move came too late to rescue developer Olympia and York.

June 5, 1992

Huge insurance losses at Lloyd's meant that its Names would have to foot the bill – estimates showed that Names would have to find an average of more than £60,000 each.

"It's this year's group photo for Lloyd's Names!"

June 8, 1992

Some doubt was cast over the veracity of some of the sources in Andrew Morton's book about Princess Diana.

"... Why, only six years ago I was chatting at the Guard's Polo Club to a waiter whose mother worked part-time for a catering company that supplied smoked salmon to a thrash Charles and Di were at!"

June 9, 1992

Prince Charles was reported to be deeply upset at the publication of Andrew Morton's book about Princess Diana which suggested that Charles had never really loved his wife and was the cause of her unhappiness.

"Well, Charles, I suggest you get someone to kiss you. You won't be able to play polo like that!"

June 10, 1992

The Environment Secretary was the senior British representative at the Earth Summit in Rio.

"They must have liked your Michael Howard, usually they only shrink the head!"

June 11, 1992

After months of severe drought, one day of storms in London brought up to two and a half inches of rain and severe flooding.

" 'Ello, 'ello, don't you know there's a hosepipe ban, sir?"

June 12, 1992

Home Secretary Kenneth Clarke warned the Association of Chief Police Officers that tact and discretion were needed when dealing with minor offences committed by "law-abiding classes" to retain their faith in the police.

". . . And remember, the next stupid fat berk who's parked his car badly could be Kenneth Clarke!"

June 15, 1992

Jeffrey Archer received a life peerage in the Queen's Birthday Honours.

"Why can't Lord Archer come into the Grill like everybody else?"

June 19, 1992

Muhamed Saeed, a fake doctor who prescribed shampoo by the spoonful and suppositories to be taken orally during 30 years of illegal practice in Britain, was jailed for five years. The true Dr Saeed was flown from Pakistan to give evidence against the man who had assumed his identity.

"Still taking a spoonful of shampoo for your gout, Carruthers?"

June 21, 1992

London Zoo was
threatened with closure.

JAK

"When Howard said he was going to rescue something from the Zoo, I thought it would be
more cuddly"

Monica Seles was criticised for her loud grunt while serving at Wimbledon. London Zoo remained under threat of closure.

"Sounds nothing like Monica Seles!"

June 25, 1992

Doctors at a medical conference discussed the question of GPs providing 24-hour cover.

"Well goodbye, Mr Smith, and try to stay alive till 10 a.m. tomorrow!"

June 26, 1992

Lloyd's Chairman David Coleridge faced hostility at the annual general meeting from Names who had made substantial losses.

"It's the safest way for the Chairman to leave these days!"

June 29, 1992

After a successful run Jeremy Bates failed to secure the point which would have put him through to the quarter finals at Wimbledon.

"Is it true, if Jeremy Bates gets through to the next round, he's going to be stuffed and put in the British Museum?"

French lorry drivers set up road blocks throughout France to protest at a new penalty points system for motoring misdemeanours.

"Not bad, any day and the asparagus will be ready to pick!"

July 6, 1992

The continued blockage of French roads by lorry drivers and sympathisers led to delays for British holiday travellers.

"P&O Ferries announce, in view of the French situation, and the need for surprise, motorists are not being told the time of departure, destination, or landing beach!"

July 7, 1992

A bizarre claim that Hitler's bones – plus those of his wife Eva Braun, propaganda minister Josef Goebbels and his wife and six children – had been found near Magdeberg in eastern Germany was written off by historians as yet another Hitler hoax.

"Don't throw it away Albert, it could be von Ribbentrop or somebody!"

Dentists voted to refuse any new NHS patients in response to Health Minister Virginia Bottomley's plan to restructure payments for dental treatment.

"I'm sorry Mrs Bottomley, I can't understand what you're screaming about!"

July 9, 1992

A new Health White Paper was published.

"... Also any rises for top people will be linked to their weight, their smoking, their drinking and how far they jog!"